I Can Cook!

MEXICAN FOOD

Wendy
Blaxland

A+

Smart Apple Media
P.O. Box 3263
Mankato, MN, 56002

First published in 2011 by
MACMILLAN EDUCATION AUSTRALIA PTY LTD
15–19 Claremont St, South Yarra, Australia 3141

Visit our website at www.macmillan.com.au or go directly to www.macmillanlibrary.com.au

Associated companies and representatives throughout the world.

Copyright text © Wendy Blaxland 2011

Library of Congress Cataloging-in-Publication Data

Blaxland, Wendy.
  Mexican food / Wendy Blaxland.
     p. cm. — (I can cook!)
  Includes index.
  Summary:"Describes historical, cultural, and geographical factors that have influenced the cuisine of Mexico.
  Includes recipes to create Mexican food"—Provided by publisher.
  ISBN 978-1-59920-668-4 (library binding)
  1. Cooking, Mexican—Juvenile literature. 2. Food—Mexico—History—Juvenile literature. 3. Cookbooks. I. Title.
  TX716.M4B57 2012
  641.5972—dc22

                    2011005444

Publisher: Carmel Heron
Commissioning Editor: Niki Horin
Managing Editor: Vanessa Lanaway
Editor: Laura Jeanne Gobal
Proofreaders: Georgina Garner; Kirstie Innes–Will
Designer: Stella Vassiliou
Page Layout: Stella Vassiliou
Photo Researcher: Claire Armstrong (management: Debbie Gallagher)
Illustrators: Jacki Sosenko; Guy Holt (map, 7, 9); Gregory Baldwin (map icons, 9)
Production Controller: Vanessa Johnson

Manufactured in China by Macmillan Production (Asia) Ltd.
Kwun Tong, Kowloon, Hong Kong
Supplier Code: CP March 2011

Acknowledgments

The author would like to thank the following for their generous help and expert advice: Emeritus Professor Eugene Anderson, University of California;
Pedro C. Chan, Mexvic, Victoria; Yim Ho, chef, Café Pacifico, Sydney; Wayne Olson, Reference Librarian, U.S. National Agricultural Library; Lynne Olver,
editor, FoodTimeline; Mireya Reyes Alvarez, Sydney; and Dena Saulsbury-Monaco, cook and librarian, Montreal.

Contents

Glossary Words

When a word is printed in **bold**, it is explained in the Glossary on page 31.

Cooking Tips

Safety Warning

Ask an adult for help when you see this red oven mitt on a recipe.

How To

Cooking techniques are explained in small boxes with this handprint.

I Can Cook!

Cooking is a rewarding and lifelong skill. With some basic cooking knowledge, a little practice, and great recipes, you can cook entire meals! Cooking for your family and friends is a fun activity, and a mouthwatering meal can take you to places that you have never been. Are you ready to have fun cooking—and eating?

A World of Food

Every day, people all over the world cook delicious and **nutritious** meals. What they cook depends not only on the ingredients available to them, but also on their country's food **culture** or cooking style. A country's style of cooking is shaped over time by its culture, **economy**, **climate**, and the land itself.

Cook Your Way Around the World

You can explore the great cuisines of the world in your own kitchen. The special flavors and wonderful aromas of a country's food culture come from fresh ingredients and particular spices or herbs, which you can find in your local supermarket or a specialty store. Share with your family and friends authentic dishes from different countries that look great and taste even better.

You can cook mouthwatering food from different countries by following a few simple steps. Some recipes involve combining just a couple of ingredients!

Mexican Food

Mexican food is known for its intense, varied flavors, wide use of spices, and rich, colorful ingredients. It blends local cooking styles and ingredients with European ones. Mexican food is just as fun to cook and eat as it looks!

Spicy or Sweet?

Mexico is the birthplace of chocolate, vanilla, and a whole range of chilies, as well as corn, beans, and tomatoes. Spain and France introduced their taste for meat, garlic, and onions to Mexico, resulting in a vibrant cooking style that features simple snacks, such as burritos, and complex sauces, called *moles*.

Cooking Mexican Food At Home

Some Mexican dishes are very simple and can easily be made at home. Guacamole, for example, needs hardly more than avocados and tomatoes. This book has seven recipes that you can follow to cook a meal on your own or with a little help from an adult. Some of the recipes don't even involve cooking! The recipes can be adapted to suit special **diets**, too.

Mexico is located in North America, immediately south of the United States.

Corn is **native** to North and South America. It is a favorite street food in Mexico, eaten roasted and straight off the cob.

Traditions and Styles

Mexican cooking **traditions** and styles developed from early **civilizations**, such as the Maya (250–900) and Aztec (1100–1521), and were later heavily influenced by the Spanish.

Corn (top), beans (left), and chilies (right) are three ingredients that are important in Mexican cooking.

Blending Vibrant Cultures

The most important Mayan foods were corn, beans, and pumpkins, along with wild game, fruit, and fish, with flavors from chilies, chocolate, and vanilla. The Aztecs used the same foods, particularly corn, but added tomatoes and turkeys. They also ate **protein**-rich insects.

In the 1520s, the Spanish (and later the French and other Europeans), who conquered Mexico in the 1500s, brought new ingredients to the country, such as wheat, beef, pork, cheese, garlic, and onions. Later influences came from the Caribbean and Portugal. Today, Mexican food is a vibrant blend of European and **Native American** cooking styles.

Regional Food

Each Mexican region has a distinct cooking style and delicious specialties made from local ingredients cooked with native and introduced spices and flavorings. The map below breaks Mexico up into six main regions and discusses the ingredients and special foods that are popular in each.

Tortillas

No Mexican meal is complete without tortillas, which are made from wheat or ground corn. Tortillas can be used to wrap tacos and enchiladas, as "plates" for *tostadas* and as "scoops" for *totopos*. They can even be dried and ground into flour to make *gorditas*, or dumplings.

Central

Central Mexico's food combines Aztec ingredients, such as corn, pumpkin, and chili, with Spanish meat- and wheat-based cooking. Shredded meat dishes include pork *carnitas* (braised or roasted) and *barbacoa* (slow-cooked meat). Special occasions call for *pozole* (pictured), a soup or stew of dried corn and meat.

Yucatán Peninsula

Many Yucatán baked chicken and pork dishes (pictured) use fruit-based sauces rather than chili, often flavored with annatto seeds, oranges, garlic, and pepper. The Maya here are traditionally beekeepers and make honey-sweetened cakes, including *rosca de miel*, and honey-based drinks, such as *balché*.

North

Northern Mexico's Spanish-influenced food includes dishes made from local goat meat and beef, such as *carne asada* (thinly sliced, spicy, grilled beef, pictured). Large, wheat-based tortillas are used here to make burritos.

West

The mountainous state of Jalisco specializes in *birria* (pictured), a dish of goat meat in a spicy chili sauce.

Southeast

Fiery Caribbean-influenced recipes include spicy dishes, such as *arroz con pollo* (rice, vegetables, and chicken). Coastal Veracruz serves *pescado a la Veracruzana* (pictured), which is fish topped with a hot chili, olive, and tomato sauce.

Oaxaca

Oaxaca is famous for its *moles*, celebratory dishes cooked with complex sauces containing up to thirty ingredients, including peanuts and cocoa. Other Oaxacan specialties include tamales (steamed snacks with meat wrapped in corn husks or leaves, pictured), *tlayudas* (crispy tortillas with refried beans, shredded meat, and salad) and Oaxacan cheese.

UNITED STATES OF AMERICA

NORTH

CENTRAL

WEST

SOUTHEAST

OAXACA

YUCATÁN PENINSULA

Gulf of Mexico

CUBA

BELIZE

GUATEMALA

HONDURAS

EL SALVADOR

NICARAGUA

Pacific Ocean

Mexican Food Basics

Mexican Ingredients

Mexican food relies as much on the meat and cheese introduced by the Spanish as it does on native ingredients, such as chocolate, vanilla, corn, beans, and, that Mexican must-have, fiery chilies.

Meat

Northern Mexican cooks enjoy beef, venison, and goat, while southern Mexican cooks prefer pork and chicken.

Seafood

Fish and other seafood, such as shrimp, are important foods in coastal states bordering the Pacific Ocean and the Gulf of Mexico.

Dairy Products

Dairy products, such as cheese, are popular in southern Mexico.

Fruit

Mexican markets blaze with brilliantly colored fruit. Juicy oranges and sweet limes jostle with watermelons, pineapples, mangoes, guavas, and custard apples.

Staple Foods

Corn is such an important **staple food** in Mexico that it was once considered sacred. Wheat is commonly used in the north. Beans are another important staple food and are often paired with rice especially in the sout

Vegetables

Tomatoes, cucumbers, corn, pumpkins, bell peppers, and chilies are popular vegetables.

Landscapes and Climates

Mexico's produce grows largely on **volcanic** soil in **tropical** and **temperate** climates. The country's landscapes include arid deserts, swampy lowlands, long coastlines, and two great mountain ranges enclosing a high central plateau. The map below shows which areas of the country Mexico's produce comes from.

Nopales

Prickly pear cactuses are farmed for their large fleshy paddles, or *nopales*, which are eaten as a vegetable. Cooks use gloves and take great care when shaving off the spines before cutting the flesh of the cactus into chunks. Green or purple *nopales* have a sticky juice and taste like raw beans.

Hunters catch animals, such as deer, in the northern mountains. Many different wild animals are used for food.

Wheat is grown in northern and central Mexico.

Pigs are raised all over Mexico for pork and lard (pig fat), which is used to flavor dishes.

Rice is grown on the swampy east coast around the Gulf of Mexico.

Farmers raise cattle for beef in northern and central Mexico.

Waters off the long coastlines provide fish, such as bonito, and other seafood, including shrimp and crabs.

Corn, beans, and sugarcane come from central and southern Mexico.

Fruit and vegetables, particularly tropical crops, are grown in the center and south.

Poultry is found everywhere, but especially in the center and south.

UNITED STATES OF AMERICA

NORTH

CENTRAL

WEST

SOUTHEAST

OAXACA

Gulf of Mexico

Pacific Ocean

YUCATÁN PENINSULA

CUBA

BELIZE

GUATEMALA   HONDURAS

Cooking Basics

Equipment

Having the right equipment to cook with is very important. Here are some of the most common items needed in the kitchen.

Potato mashers break up food.

Frying pans fry or brown food.

Sieves separate and break up food.

Spatulas lift and turn food.

Cook pasta, rice, soups, and stews in saucepans.

Big knives chop. Small knives cut and peel. Butter knives spread. Serrated knives slice.

Oven mitts protect hands from heat.

Baking pans hold food in an oven.

Peelers remove the skins from fruit and vegetables.

Forks hold, stir, or prick food.

Whisks beat food to add air and make it light.

Tongs are used to handle hot food.

Measuring cups and spoons measure ingredients accurately.

Cutting boards provide safe surfaces for cutting food.

Blenders chop ingredients, mix food, and make smooth sauces and soups

Spoons mix and stir. Wooden spoons prevent scratched pans. Slotted spoons let liquid drain away.

Graters shave thin slices from food, such as cheese.

Colanders drain liquids.

Mixers mix food quickly.

Bowls hold food for mixing.

Cooking Basics

Weight, Volume, Temperature, and Special Diets

It is important to use the right amount of ingredients, cook at the correct heat, and be aware of people with special dietary needs.

Weight and Volume

The weight and volume of ingredients can be measured with a weighing scale or with measuring cups and spoons. Convert them using this table. Measure dry ingredients so that they are level across the top of the spoon or cup without packing them down.

Recipe Measurement		Weight	Volume
1 cup	1 cup	8 ounces	250 ml
½ cup	½ cup	4 ounces	125 ml
2 tablespoons	2 tablespoons	1 ounce	30 ml
1 teaspoon	1 teaspoon	0.16 ounce	4.7 ml

Temperature

Fahrenheit and Celsius are two different ways of measuring temperature. Oven dials may show the temperature in either Fahrenheit or Celsius. Use lower temperatures in gas or convection ovens.

Oven Temperature	Celsius	Fahrenheit
Slow	150°	300°
Moderately slow	160°–170°	320°–340°
Moderate	180°	350°
Moderately hot	190°	375°
Hot	200°	400°
Very hot	220°–240°	430°–470°

Special Diets

Some people follow special diets because of personal or religious beliefs about what they should eat. Others must not eat certain foods because they are **allergic** to them.

Diet	What It Means	Symbol
Allergy-specific	Some people's bodies react to a certain food as if it were poison. They may die from eating even a tiny amount of this food. Nuts, eggs, milk, strawberries, and even chocolate may cause allergic reactions.	
Halal	**Muslims** eat only food prepared according to strict religious guidelines. This is called halal food.	
Kosher	**Jews** eat only food prepared according to strict religious guidelines. This is called kosher food.	
Vegan	Vegans eat nothing from animals, including dairy products, eggs and honey.	
Vegetarian	Vegetarians eat no animal products and may or may not eat dairy products, eggs and honey.	

Safety and Hygiene

Be safe in the kitchen by staying alert and using equipment correctly when cooking. Practicing good food hygiene means you always serve clean, germ-free food. Follow the handy tips below!

13

Be Organized

Hungry? Organized cooks eat sooner! First, read the recipe. Next, take out the equipment and ingredients you'll need and follow the stages set out in the recipe. Straighten up and clean as you go. While your food cooks, wash up, sweep the kitchen floor, and empty the garbage.

eat

ace boiling saucepans toward the back of the ove with handles turned inward. Keep your nds and face away from steam and switch t equipment off as soon as you have finished sing it. Use oven mitts to pick up hot pots and t them down on heatproof surfaces. Always eck that food is cool enough to eat.

Emergencies

All kitchens should have a fire blanket, fire extinguisher, and first-aid box.

Food Hygiene

To avoid spreading germs, wash your hands well and keep coughs and sneezes away from food. Use fresh ingredients and always store food that spoils easily, such as meat and fish, in the refrigerator.

Electricity

Use electrical equipment only with an adult's help. Switch the power off before unplugging any equipment and keep it away from water.

Knives

When cutting food with a knife, cut away from yourself and onto a nonslip surface, such as a suitable cutting board.

Huevos Rancheros

Many Mexicans work hard on farms and huevos rancheros, or ranch-style eggs, were originally served on these farms as a mid-morning meal. Today, these delicious eggs on tortillas, served with salsa, a tomato and chili sauce, are popular around the world for breakfast or as a snack.

MAKES: 2 servings

PREPARATION TIME: 10 minutes

COOKING TIME: 10 minutes

FOOD VALUES: About 240 **calories**, 12 grams of fat, 11 grams of protein, and 21 grams of **carbohydrates** per serving.

SPECIAL DIETS: Suitable for vegetarian, nut-free, kosher, and halal diets. For **gluten-free** diets, use gluten-free flour; and for vegan diets, use 2 tablespoons of refried beans instead of eggs.

Equipment

- Large frying pan
- Spatula
- 2 damp paper towels
- 2 serving plates

Ingredients

- 3 teaspoons of vegetable oil (canola or sunflower)
- 1 clove of garlic, finely chopped
- ½ of a white onion, finely chopped
- ½ of a green chili, finely chopped (optional)
- 3 large tomatoes, finely chopped
- ½ of a green, yellow, or red bell pepper, finely chopped
- 4 eggs
- 2 tortillas
- 1 tablespoon of chopped cilantro

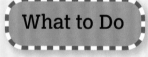

What to Do

Recipe Variations

Add warm refried beans (see pages 16–17) or a slice of ham to the tortilla before the eggs. Top the dish with grated cheese.

Fry the garlic, onion, chili, and vegetables gently in oil in the frying pan on medium heat. Stir the ingredients well until the mixture thickens.

Carefully crack the eggs onto the vegetables. Cook until the yolks are almost firm or how you like them.

Ask an adult for help with using the stove and microwave. You might also like to wear gloves when handling the chili.

While the eggs are cooking, put the tortillas between the damp paper towels on a plate and heat them for 30 seconds in the microwave.

Remove the tortillas from the microwave and discard the paper towels. Transfer one tortilla to the other plate. Using the spatula, slide two eggs and half the sauce out of the frying pan and onto each tortilla.

Sprinkle half of the chopped cilantro onto each serving. Enjoy!

Let's Cook!

MAKES: 4 servings

PREPARATION TIME: 10 minutes

COOKING TIME: 15 minutes

FOOD VALUES: About 234 calories, 9 g of fat, 14 g of protein, and 38 g of carbohydrates per serving.

SPECIAL DIETS: Suitable for vegan, vegetarian, nut-free, gluten-free, kosher, and halal diets.

Refried Beans

Beans have always been important in Mexican cooking, especially to poorer families. The country has many native beans, both plain or speckled, and in a variety of colors—black, white, brown, red, even purple. Beans can be cooked in Mexican soups, stews, and fritters. However, refried mashed beans are probably the tastiest.

Equipment

- Colander
- Large saucepan
- Wooden spoon
- Potato masher
- Serving plate and bowl

Ingredients

- 3 cups of cooked beans (any kind)
- 1 tablespoon of vegetable oil (canola or sunflower)
- 1 onion, roughly chopped
- 2 cubes of vegetable bouillon (or 2 teaspoons of bouillon powder)
- ½ cup of hot water
- Salt, to taste
- 4 tortillas

What to Do

1 Put the beans in a colander and rinse them until the water runs clear.

2 Pour the oil into the saucepan, then gently fry the chopped onion on medium heat until it turns clear, but not brown.

3 Gradually add the beans to the onion.

Ask an adult for help with using the stove.

Next, crumble the vegetable bouillon cubes into the bean mixture, then add the water and stir.

Remove the saucepan from the stove and place it on a heatproof surface. Mash the bean mixture until it forms a paste (about 5 minutes). Add salt to taste.

Serve the refried beans on their own or on tortillas.

Let's Cook!

Guacamole

Guacamole is an avocado-based dip that dates back to the Aztecs. Mexicans have eaten avocados for at least 10,000 years. Avocados are actually large berries with a big seed inside and are full of vitamins, fiber, and good fats. Guacamole is traditionally made and served in a *molcajete* (volcanic stone mortar and pestle) with fresh, warm tortillas.

Equipment

- Cutting board
- Small, sharp knife
- Small bowl
- Fork (or potato masher)
- Citrus juicer
- Tablespoon

Ingredients

- 1 ripe tomato, finely chopped
- ¼ of a medium-size onion (white or red), finely chopped
- Handful of fresh cilantro leaves, roughly chopped
- 1 chili, deseeded and finely chopped
- 1 lime
- 2 ripe avocados
- Salt and pepper, to taste
- Tortillas, cornchips, crackers, or vegetable sticks, to serve

What to Do

Set aside a little of the chopped tomato, onion, and cilantro to use as a **garnish**. Mash the rest and the chopped chili in the small bowl. Add salt and pepper if you wish.

Roll the lime on the cutting board, pressing down hard to free the juice inside. Cut the lime in half and squeeze the juice out with the citrus juicer. Add the pulp to the juice.

Cut the avocados in half. Remove the seeds and any discolored flesh and throw these away.

Recipe Variations

Garnish with crispy bacon bits or a little low-fat sour cream.

Spread the guacamole on toast and top with smoked salmon.

Ask an adult for help with using the knife. You might also like to wear gloves when handling the chili.

4 Using the tablespoon, scoop the remaining avocado flesh out of the skin and into the bowl. Mash the flesh with the fork.

5 Add the lime juice to the bowl and mix. Add a little salt and pepper to taste.

6 Garnish the guacamole with the onion, tomatoes, and cilantro that were set aside. Serve with fresh tortillas, corn chips, crackers, or vegetable sticks.

MAKES: 2 burritos

PREPARATION TIME: 10 minutes

FOOD VALUES: About 280 calories, 18 g of fat, 13 g of protein, and 39 g of carbohydrates per burrito.

SPECIAL DIETS: Suitable for nut-free diets. For vegan diets, avoid meat and cheese; for vegetarian diets, avoid meat; for gluten-free diets, use gluten-free tortillas; and for kosher and halal diets, use certified foods.

Burritos

No Mexican meal is complete without wheat-flour tortillas. Burritos, or "little donkeys," are just tortillas wrapped around a simple filling, such as refried beans or meat. Some say the burrito was created by a Mexican taco seller who traveled on a donkey and kept his tacos warm by wrapping them in tortillas. Burritos are popular in northern Mexico.

What to Do

Equipment

- 2 damp paper towels (if using microwave)
- Serving plate
- Large frying pan (if warming tortillas on stove)
- Tablespoon

Ingredients

- 2 tortillas
- ½ cup of your favorite salsa (try the huevos rancheros sauce on pages 14–15)
- ½ cup of your choice of filling (try the refried beans on pages 16–17 or shredded cooked chicken)
- 1 ripe tomato, cut into small cubes
- ½ of a bell pepper, cut into small cubes
- 2 ounces of your favorite cheese, grated
- 1 tablespoon of fresh cilantro, finely chopped
- ½ of a lime

1

Put the tortillas between damp paper towels on a plate and warm them for 30 seconds in the microwave. Discard the paper towels after. You can also warm the tortillas in the frying pan on medium heat and then transfer them to the plate.

2

Spoon half of the salsa in a line across the middle of one tortilla, stopping about 3 inches from one end and 1 inch from the other.

3

Sprinkle half of the filling, tomato, bell pepper, cheese, and cilantro over the salsa. Don't overfill the tortilla. Squeeze a dash of lime juice on top.

Recipe Variations

Replace the tomato, bell pepper, cilantro, and cheese with corn kernels, cucumber, and lettuce, and drizzle some balsamic vinegar over the filling instead of lime juice.

Heat the burritos for 30 seconds to melt the cheese before adding the vegetables.

Ask an adult for help with using the stove or microwave.

4 Fold the bottom flap of the tortilla up over the end of the filling.

5 Fold one side of the tortilla firmly across the filling and the bottom flap.

6 Wrap the other side of the tortilla around the entire burrito to hold it together. Repeat steps 2–6 with the remaining tortilla. Enjoy!

Mexican Fruit Salad

Mexican markets are full of color, especially the stalls selling fruit salad. On hot days, families enjoy bowls filled with chunks of red watermelon and strawberries, yellow pineapple and mango, and more. A Mexican fruit salad may also include vegetables, such as jicama (a Mexican turnip), and even cucumber! A little lime juice and chili powder add a distinctive Mexican touch to the fruit salad.

MAKES: 4 servings

PREPARATION TIME: 15 minutes

FOOD VALUES: About 70 calories, 5 g of protein, and 12 g of carbohydrates per serving. No fat.

SPECIAL DIETS: Suitable for vegan, vegetarian, gluten-free, kosher, and halal diets. For nut-free diets, don't add nuts.

Recipe Variations

Use any combination of fruit that you like.

Add yogurt and honey or a little chopped mint for a different flavor.

Equipment

- Serving bowl
- Cutting board
- Small, sharp knife
- Citrus juicer
- Salad servers
- 4 small bowls
- 4 tablespoons

Ingredients

- 1 ripe pineapple, cut into chunks
- ¼ of a watermelon, cut into chunks
- 1 cucumber, cut into chunks
- 20 strawberries, halved
- 1 mango, cut into chunks
- 1 lime
- A pinch of salt
- A pinch of chili powder (optional)
- Handful of seeds or nuts (optional)

What to Do

1 Put all of the chunks of fruit and cucumber into the serving bowl.

2 Roll the lime on the cutting board, pressing down hard to free the juice inside. Cut the lime in half and squeeze the juice out with the citrus juicer. Add the pulp to the juice.

Ask an adult for help with using the knife.

3 Add the lime juice and salt to the fruit salad and toss gently with the salad servers.

4 If using, sprinkle a little chili powder over the salad.

5 Scatter some nuts over the salad if you wish. Chill the fruit salad in the refrigerator or serve it immediately in bowls with spoons.

Let's Cook!

Makes: 2 mugs of hot chocolate

Preparation time: 15 minutes

Food values: About 150 calories, 6 g of fat, 8 g of protein, and 21 g of carbohydrates per mug.

Special diets: Suitable for vegetarian, nut-free, gluten-free, kosher, and halal diets. For vegan diets, use soy milk.

Hot Chocolate

Did you know chocolate was at first drunk, and not eaten, by the Maya and Aztecs? They ground the beans of the cacao tree, from which chocolate is made, into a paste, dissolved it in water, and added a little chili or vanilla. Cacao beans were so valuable to the Maya and Aztecs that they were also often used as money. Today, chocolate is used in both savory and sweet Mexican dishes.

Equipment

- Mortar and pestle
- Measuring spoons
- Airtight container
- Small bowl
- Small saucepan
- Whisk
- 2 mugs

Ingredients

- 1 teaspoon of Mexican *piloncillo* (or dark brown sugar)
- 3 ounces of Mexican semisweet chocolate, broken into pieces (or a hot chocolate powder)
- ½ teaspoon of ground cinnamon
- Small pinch of salt
- 1 teaspoon of Mexican vanilla extract
- 2½ cups of milk

What to Do

1 If necessary, grind the *piloncillo* to a powder using the mortar and pestle. Place 1 teaspoon of *piloncillo* in the bowl. Put any extra *piloncillo* in an airtight container and store for another time.

2 Put the *piloncillo*, chocolate pieces, cinnamon, salt, vanilla extract, and milk in the saucepan. If using chocolate powder, keep a little aside for later.

Stir the liquid in a circular motion, with increasing speed.

Recipe Variations

Instead of ground cinnamon and vanilla extract, drop a cinnamon stick, vanilla bean, and three cloves into the milk while heating for a more complex, spicy taste. Take them out before you start whisking.

Ask an adult for help with using the mortar and pestle, and stove.

3

Heat the ingredients in the saucepan on medium to low heat. Make sure it does not boil. **Whisk** until the chocolate has melted and all of the ingredients are well combined.

4

Remove the saucepan from the stove and carefully pour the hot chocolate into the mugs. Sprinkle a little chocolate powder over the froth, and serve.

Pan de Muertos

Pan de muertos is a special sweetbread baked for Día de los Muertos (see pages 28–29), the Day of the Dead. It is made from wheat flour and is usually decorated with dough that has been twisted into the shape of bones and skulls. You can make *pan de muertos* at home.

MAKES: 1 large loaf

PREPARATION TIME: 50 minutes plus 2 hours rising time

COOKING TIME: 40 minutes

FOOD VALUES: About 250 calories, 9 g of fat, 5 g of protein, and 32 g of carbohydrates per slice.

SPECIAL DIETS: Suitable for vegetarian, nut-free, kosher, and halal diets. For gluten-free diets, use gluten-free flour or gluten-free pastry. Not suitable for vegan diets.

Recipe Variations

Make three small loaves with different decorations.

Equipment

- Large mixing bowl
- Measuring cup and spoons
- 2 small saucepans
- Wooden spoon
- Large breadboard (optional)
- Plastic wrap
- Baking pan, sprinkled with flour
- Pastry brush

Ingredients

FOR BREAD

- 5–6 cups of plain flour (plus extra for flouring and kneading)
- 2 packets of dry yeast (or 2 tablespoons)
- 1 teaspoon of salt
- 1 tablespoon of whole aniseeds
- ½ cup of white sugar (plus extra to sprinkle)
- ½ cup of milk
- ½ cup of water
- ½ cup of butter
- 4 eggs

FOR GLAZE

- ½ cup of sugar
- ⅓ cup of fresh orange juice
- 2 tablespoons of grated orange peel

What to Do

1 First, combine 1½ cups of the flour with the yeast, salt, aniseeds, and sugar. Mix thoroughly.

2 Next, heat the milk, water, and butter in one saucepan on medium heat until it is close to boiling. Stir this warm liquid into the flour mixture and mix thoroughly.

3 Crack the eggs into the flour mixture and combine. Add the remaining flour gradually and stir until a smooth, shiny, and elastic dough forms.

How To: Knead

Use the heels of your hands to press down on the dough and push it away from you, then fold it back over itself. Turn the dough a little and repeat until it feels smooth and elastic.

Ask an adult for help with kneading and resting the dough, and using the oven.

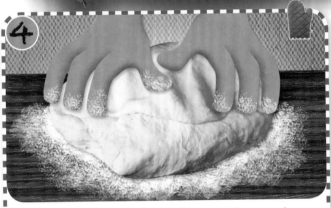

4 Coat your hands and a surface, such as a clean kitchen counter or breadboard, lightly with flour. **Knead** the dough on this surface for about 10 minutes.

5 Lightly grease the empty bowl with some butter and place the dough in the bowl in a warm spot (about 70°F) to rise. Cover it with plastic wrap to stop it from drying out. The dough should double in size after about 1½–2 hours.

6 Tear off about ¼ of the dough and shape the remainder into a round loaf. Place the loaf on the baking pan. Make "bones" by rolling some of the leftover dough into two strips with knobby ends. Put them on the loaf in an "X" shape. Place a small ball of dough, representing a skull, in the center of the "X". Let the loaf rise for 1 hour.

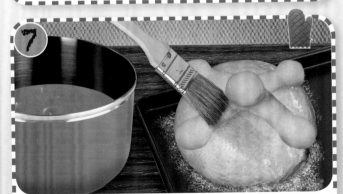

7 While waiting, set the oven to 350°F. Make the glaze by boiling the sugar, orange juice, and orange peel in the other saucepan for 2 minutes. Using the pastry brush, coat the top of the loaf with the glaze, then sprinkle some sugar over it. Bake the loaf for 40 minutes until golden brown.

A Mexican Food Celebration: Día de los Muertos

Día de los Muertos, or the Day of the Dead, is a unique Mexican festival that honors the dead. It is a time for families to come together, and remember and celebrate loved ones who have died.

What Is Día de los Muertos?

Día de los Muertos is celebrated on November 1 and 2. The first day honors children and babies who have died, while the second day is for adults. Día de los Muertos is not a sad festival, but a happy one that encourages the living and the souls of the dead to meet again.

How Is Día de los Muertos Celebrated?

Mexican families build elaborate altars at home and fill them with offerings of their loved ones' favorite foods and possessions to encourage their souls to visit. Families gather in cemeteries in the evening and redecorate the graves with food, drinks, and flowers, especially marigolds. They may have a picnic by candlelight and share funny stories about their loved ones. There may even be fireworks!

Dolls that look like dressed-up skeletons are sold for Día de los Muertos.

Many families decorate the graves of their loved ones with marigolds.

Food

Family members prepare the favorite foods of those whose souls will be returning for Día de los Muertos. They believe the souls will enjoy the food through its aroma, while their living family members eat the actual food. Water is provided for thirsty souls, as well as corn-based drinks, such as *atole*.

Bakers make a special sweet bread called *pan de muertos*, or the bread of the dead, decorated with bones or skulls made from dough (see pages 26–27). In the markets you'll find mounds of brightly colored sugar or chocolate skulls and pumpkin sweets.

Celebrations In Pátzcuaro

On November 1 in Pátzcuaro, in the state of Michoacán, children "steal" food, which is then cooked to feed the community. At midnight on November 2, the townspeople carry candles in winged boats called *mariposas* (butterflies) to the island cemetery in the middle of a lake and spend the night there.

Calaveras de azucar (sugar skulls) are a hard sugar candy shaped like little skulls.

Try This!

Cooking is a creative skill you can enjoy every day. Try these activities and learn more about cooking Mexican food.

- Find out what insects are sold as food at Mexican country markets. Are you willing to try a recipe that includes grasshoppers or grubs?

- Celebrate a special Mexican holiday by preparing food in the colors of the Mexican flag, such as green salsa verde and red tomato salsa on Mexican *arroz blanco* (white rice).

- Plant your own Mexican chili garden with chili plants in different colors. Explore recipes that use them.

- Collect pictures of the different kinds of Mexican chilies. Start a chili dictionary and rate the chilies according to how hot they are.

- Find a recipe for the candy skulls made for the Day of the Dead. Try it!

- What spices are used in Mexican cooking? Get online and find recipes that use them.

- Check your nearest supermarket or Mexican specialty store for *nopales*. Find a recipe that includes them and cook it for your family.

- Using the internet, find out as much as you can about the kinds of beans grown in Mexico.

Glossary

allergic
having an allergy, or a bad reaction to certain foods

calories
units measuring the amount of energy food provides

carbohydrates
substances that provide the body with energy

civilizations
the cultures or ways of life of certain societies or countries during a period of time

climate
the general weather conditions of an area

culture
the ways of living that a group of people has developed over time

diets
foods and drinks normally consumed by different people or groups of people

economy
the system of trade by which a country makes and uses its wealth

garnish
a small amount of a certain food used to add flavor or color to a dish

gluten
a protein found in wheat and some other grains that makes dough springy

Jews
people who follow the religion of Judaism

Muslims
people who follow the religion of Islam

native
living or growing naturally in a place

Native American
relating to the indigenous peoples of North, South, or Central America, but especially of the North

nutritious
providing nutrients, or nourishment

protein
a nutrient that helps bodies grow and heal

staple food
a food that is eaten regularly and is one of the main parts of a diet

temperate
a moderate climate without extreme temperatures

traditions
patterns of behavior handed down through generations

tropical
a climate with consistently high temperatures and a lot of rain; or describing something that grows in this climate

volcanic
produced by a volcano

Index

A
allergies 12
Aztec civilization 6, 18, 24

B
burritos 5, 20–21

C
calories 14, 16, 18, 20, 22, 24, 26
carbohydrates 14, 16, 18, 20, 22, 24, 26
chocolate 5, 6, 8, 12, 24, 25, 29
climate 4, 9
culture 4, 6

D
dairy products 8, 12
Día de los Muertos 26, 28–29

E
economy 4
equipment 10–11, 14, 16, 18, 20, 22, 24, 26

F
fruit 6, 7, 8, 9, 10, 22
fruit salad 22–23

G
gluten 14, 16, 18, 20, 22, 24, 26
guacamole 5, 18–19

H
halal diets 12, 14, 16, 18, 20, 22, 24, 26
hot chocolate 24–25
huevos rancheros 14–15, 20
hygiene 13

I
ingredients 4, 5, 6, 8–9, 11, 12, 13, 14, 16, 18, 20, 22, 24, 26

K
kosher diets 12, 14, 16, 18, 20, 22, 24, 26

L
landscapes 9

M
Maya civilization 6, 24
measurements 12
meat 5, 7, 8, 13, 20

N
native foods 5, 7, 8, 16

P
pan de muertos 26–27, 29
protein 6, 14, 16, 18, 20, 22, 24, 26

R
refried beans 7, 14, 16–17, 20
regional food 7

S
safety 13, 15, 17, 19, 21, 23, 25, 27
seafood 8, 9
Spanish influence 5, 6, 7, 8
special diets 5, 12, 14, 16, 18, 20, 22, 24, 26
staple foods 8

T
temperature 12
traditions 6–7, 18

V
vegan diets 12, 14, 16, 18, 20, 22, 24, 26
vegetables 7, 8, 9, 14, 19, 22, 26
vegetarian diets 12, 14, 16, 18, 20, 22, 24, 26
volume 12

W
weight 12